D1487567

...Relationships in
... / T / 800L

Set J

Understanding
BIOMES

By Jeanne Sturm

Rourke
Educational Media

rourkeeducationalmedia.com

© 2012 Rourke Educational Media

All rights reserved. No part of this book may be reproduced or utilized in any form or by any means, electronic or mechanical including photocopying, recording, or by any information storage and retrieval system without permission in writing from the publisher.

www.rourkeeducationalmedia.com

PHOTO CREDITS:
Front Cover: © Borut Trdina; © Asterixvs; © YinYang; © Vladimir Chernyanskiy; © Dariusz Lewandowski; © Richard Carey; © Steven Love, Back Cover: © Borut Trdina; Title page © Vera Kailova; Table of contents © Mauro Pezzotta; Page 4 © szefei; Page 5 © Uryadnikov Sergey, worldswildlifewonders, szefei; Page 6 © irabel8, Diane Uhley; Page 7 © NASA, szefei, Valery Shanin, Dominik Michálek; Page 8 © Alyssia Sheikh; Page 9 © Alyssia Sheikh, Valerie Potapova; Page 10 © Graeme Shannon; Page 11 © Alyssia Sheikh; Page 12/13 © Eky Studio; Page 12 © Vera Kailova, gallimaufry; Page 13 © Eduardo Rivero, formiktopus, hagit berkovich; Page 14 © Frontpage, STILLFX; Page 15 © Ralph Loesche; Page 16 © Warren Price Photography, joyfull, Inga Nielsen; Page 17 © Mauro Pezzotta, David P. Smith; Page 18 © He-ba-mue; Page 19 © EcoPic; Page 20/21 © Matthew Jacques; Page 20 © Oleg_Mit; Page 21 © AJ Gagnon, Serg Zastavkin, Andreas Gradin; Page 22 © Stubblefield Photography, oksana.perkins; Page 23 © Paul Gana, visceralimage; Page 24/25 © Sam DCruz; Page 24 © Sam DCruz, NASA; Page 25 © Christian Musat, Cathy Keifer, bofotolux; Page 26/27 © baldovina; Page 27 © Ellen Isaacs; Page 28 © Matthijs Wetterauw; Page 29 © Darren J. Bradley; Page 30/31 © Valentin Mosichev; Page 30 © Yuriy Kulyk; Page 31 © Dirk Ercken. NOAA; Page 32/33 © holbox; Page 33 © RazvanZinica, Rudy Umans, photofun; Page 34/35 © Kostiantyn Karpenko; Page 35 © Stephen Inglis, iliuta goean, Insuratelu Gabriela Gianina; Page 36/37 © Vlad61; Page 37 © Masonjar; Page 38 © Vlad61, David Nielsam, Rich Carey; Page 39 © Vlad61, cbpix; Page 40 © NASA; Page 41 © worldswildlifewonders; Page 42 © Krzysztof Odziomek; Page 43 © Danny E Hooks; Page 44 © Yummyphotos; Page 45 © Lance O. Brown

Edited by Precious McKenzie

Cover design by Tara Raymo
Layout by Nicola Stratford, Blue Door Publishing, Florida

Library of Congress Cataloging-in-Publication Data

Sturm, Jeanne
  Understanding Biomes / Jeanne Sturm
    p. cm. -- (Let's Explore Science)
  ISBN 978-1-61741-783-2 (hard cover) (alk. paper)
  ISBN 978-1-61741-985-0 (soft cover)
  Library of Congress Control Number: 2011924828

Rourke Educational Media
Printed in the United States of America,
North Mankato, Minnesota

rourkeeducationalmedia.com

customerservice@rourkeeducationalmedia.com • PO Box 643328 Vero Beach, Florida 32964

Table of Contents

CHAPTER ONE

What Are Biomes?

What is the climate like where you live? Is it hot or cold, dry or rainy? Think about the animals and plants that are native to your area. You might not have realized it, but the climate where you live, and the plants and animals that live there, put your community in one of Earth's biomes.

Biomes are large regions on Earth with similar climates, plants, and animals. The environmental conditions in a biome—its temperature and **precipitation**—determine which plants and animals can live there.

Woolly spider monkeys of the tropical rainforest would not survive in the dry desert biome, just as the antelope of the grasslands is not adapted to conditions in a tropical rainforest.

Terrestrial biomes occur on land. These include forests, grasslands, savannahs, deserts, and tundras. **Aquatic** biomes are the freshwater and saltwater biomes. Freshwater biomes include lakes, ponds, rivers, streams, and wetlands. The largest biome on Earth, however, is composed of saltwater. It is the oceans. Together, the oceans cover about 70 percent of Earth's surface.

The evaporation of seawater from aquatic saltwater biomes provides rainwater for the plants and animals living in land biomes.

The Everglades, in Florida, is called the River of Grass. Both crocodiles and alligators inhabit its waters.

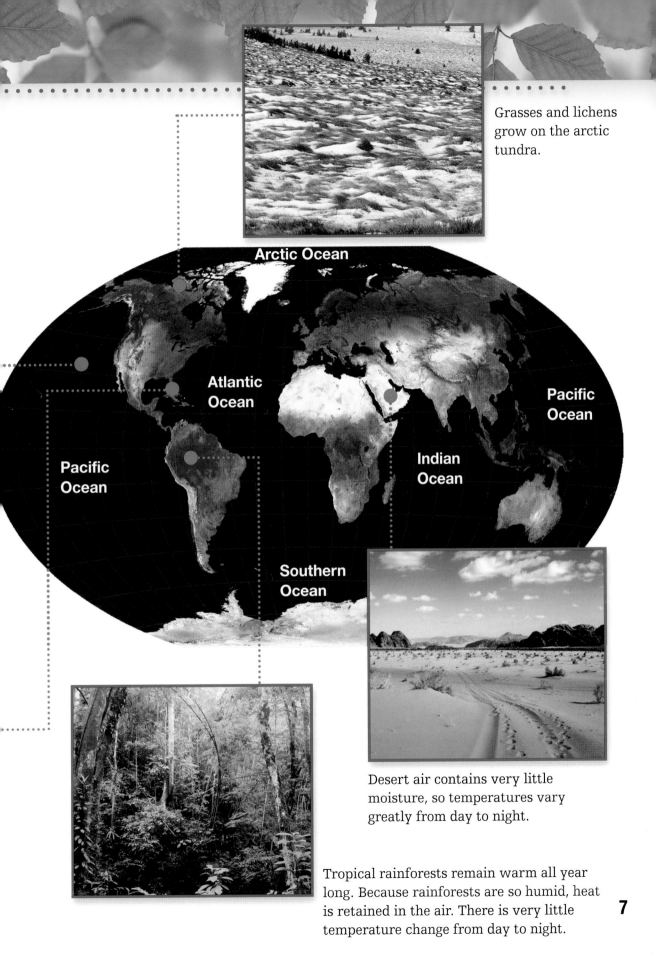

Grasses and lichens grow on the arctic tundra.

Arctic Ocean

Atlantic Ocean

Pacific Ocean

Pacific Ocean

Indian Ocean

Southern Ocean

Desert air contains very little moisture, so temperatures vary greatly from day to night.

Tropical rainforests remain warm all year long. Because rainforests are so humid, heat is retained in the air. There is very little temperature change from day to night.

7

Latitude

What causes the different biomes? One factor is **latitude**. Latitude is the distance north or south of the **equator**. We measure it in degrees. In the tropical regions near the equator there are no summer and winter seasons. Temperatures stay high throughout the year. In tropical rainforests, the continuous growing season allows for great **biodiversity**, or variety of species.

Latitude tells us how far something is north or south of the equator. The north and south poles, at 90 degrees latitude, receive the least direct rays from the Sun.

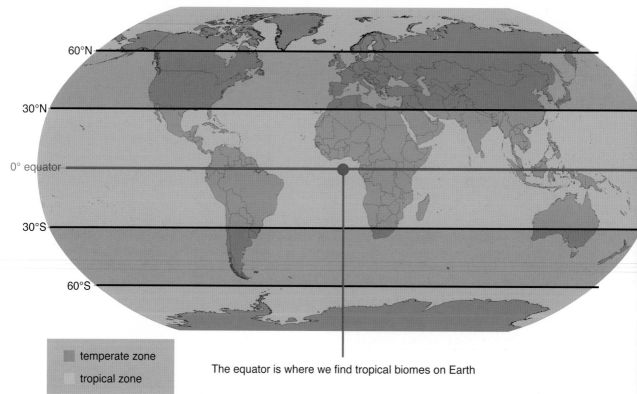

60°N

30°N

0° equator

30°S

60°S

temperate zone

tropical zone

The equator is where we find tropical biomes on Earth

As we move away from the equator, the climate becomes more moderate. In the latitudes 30 to 60 degrees north and south of the equator, we find **temperate** forests and grasslands. Most of the world's food grows in these regions.

Far from the equator, near the north and south poles, the Sun's rays are indirect and not as strong. In the arctic tundra, plants and animals are adapted to the short growing season and cold temperatures.

north pole

south pole

Altitude and Precipitation

Altitude, the height of an object above sea level, also plays a role in determining biomes. As you move higher up a mountain, the temperature gets cooler. Mount Kilimanjaro, in Africa, sits just 3 degrees south of the equator. At its base we find scrubland. Higher up the mountain are tropical rainforests teeming with life. Yet higher, we find alpine tundra, and finally at the top, a snow-covered, rocky peak.

Mount Kilimanjaro is the highest mountain in Africa. There is always snow at its peak, 19,341 feet (5,895 meters) above the African plain.

Precipitation is another important factor in determining a region's biomes. Even when two areas have similar latitudes and altitudes, their relationship to a nearby mountain range can cause them to have very different climates. On the windward side of a mountain, wind carries air masses up toward the peak. As the air rises, its temperature falls, and it drops snow or rain on the mountainside.

The air mass reaches the peak and begins to make its way down the leeward side of the mountain. The air warms as it descends, and is much drier than the land on the windward side.

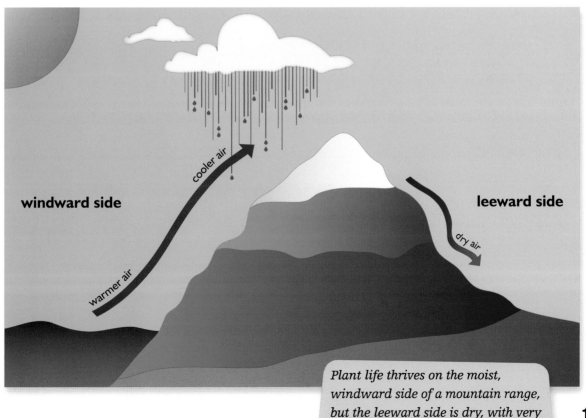

windward side

cooler air

warmer air

leeward side

dry air

Plant life thrives on the moist, windward side of a mountain range, but the leeward side is dry, with very little vegetation.

CHAPTER TWO

Forest Biomes

Tropical Rainforests

Tropical rainforests make up 20 percent of the world's forests. They cover about 6 percent of all the land on Earth, yet they are home to more than half of the planet's plant and animal species.

There are four distinct layers in the rainforest. The topmost layer is the emergent layer. Trees in the emergent layer grow as high as 200 feet (61 meters) tall. The trees receive plenty of sunlight. Monkeys, eagles, bats, and butterflies live here at the heights of the rainforest.

Blue Morpho Butterfly

4x5 FILM

220 EPT SSO

Fruit Bat

Below the emergent layer is the canopy. There is much food here to support a great variety of animal life. Snakes, toucans, and tree frogs live in the canopy layer.

Not much sunlight makes it through to the understory, the third layer of the rainforest. There is less wind in the understory, and it is more humid than the higher layers. Plants grow very large leaves, so they can absorb as much sunlight as possible.

The forest floor is dark, warm, and moist. There are very few plants, but insects, fungi, and **microorganisms** thrive.

Poison Dart Frog

Animals in the rainforest protect themselves from predators in very different ways. The Costa Rican mantis and the leaf-tailed gecko use camouflage to blend in with their surroundings. Others, including poison dart frogs, employ bright colors that warn predators to stay away.

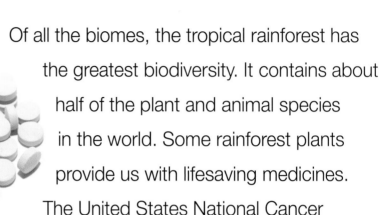

Of all the biomes, the tropical rainforest has the greatest biodiversity. It contains about half of the plant and animal species in the world. Some rainforest plants provide us with lifesaving medicines. The United States National Cancer Institute lists 3,000 plants with cancer-fighting characteristics. More than 70 percent of these plants grow in the tropical rainforest.

Deforestation is a major threat to the rainforest. In the last 50 years, people have burned or cut down about half of the world's tropical rainforests.

Tropical rainforests are called the Lungs of our Planet. They remove carbon dioxide from the atmosphere and produce 40 percent of the world's oxygen.

Deciduous Forests

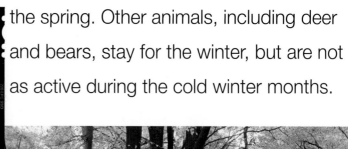

Deciduous forests lie in the **temperate** zone, further from the equator. There are four distinct seasons here: spring, summer, fall, and winter. In the fall, leaves change color and drop to the ground. Squirrels eat the nuts, seeds, and fruits the trees provide. Most of the birds here are migratory. They fly south each winter and return in the spring. Other animals, including deer and bears, stay for the winter, but are not as active during the cold winter months.

CHAPTER THREE

Desert and Tundra

Desert

Deserts are the driest biome. They receive less than 10 inches (25 centimeters) of rain each year. The Sahara Desert in Africa and the Sonoran Desert in Arizona are hot and dry deserts. They are close to the equator and remain hot all year round. There is very little moisture in the desert air. In the daytime, temperatures can reach 100 degrees Fahrenheit (38 degrees Celsius) and higher. But after sunset, without humidity to hold in the heat, the temperature can quickly fall below freezing.

Desert plants have **adaptations** that help them absorb water from the ground even when there is little water available. Some desert plants have shallow roots that spread out over a wide area. Others have a **taproot** that extends deep into the ground.

Did You Know?
Carrots do not grow in deserts but they are taproots.

North America

Europe

Asia
Gobi Desert

Africa

equator

South America

Australia

Antarctica

Sauxal Shrub

The Gobi Desert in China is a cold desert. It gets about 7 inches (18 centimeters) of rain each year. Plants adapt by growing long roots so they can absorb water from a large area and by losing their leaves during dry periods. The sauxal is a shrub that grows in the Gobi desert. It has very few leaves. In some areas, sauxals grow in groups, creating a small forest. These forests provide a habitat for desert animals and firewood for people.

Sometimes, days and weeks pass without a meal, so when the desert animals find food, they store as much of it as they can. Camels store fat in their humps. Banded Gila monsters store fat in their tails and bodies. They can survive for about three months on their stored fat.

Water is scarce in deserts. Some animals dig into dry riverbeds until they reach water. Others get their liquid from plants. But some desert rodents don't drink any water at all. Kangaroo Rats have the ability to obtain water from their diet of dry seeds!

Escaping the extreme heat is a priority. Many desert animals are nocturnal. They are active at night and sleep during the heat of the day. Some rodents go so far as to plug the entrances to their burrows to keep out the hot, desert air.

The African ground squirrel has a unique solution to the Sun's strong rays. It uses its fluffy tail as an umbrella.

Arctic Tundra

With average winter temperatures of -63 degrees Fahrenheit (-34 degrees Celsius) the arctic tundra is the coldest biome. It receives very little precipitation and its growing season lasts only 50 to 60 days. For about 8 weeks in the summer, the top layer of soil thaws. It's a very thin layer of soil; in some places it is only 3 inches (8 centimeters) deep. Below this active zone lies the permafrost. Permafrost is a permanently frozen layer of soil. Since the roots of tundra plants cannot penetrate the permafrost, they grow very close to the surface. Even so, low shrubs, reindeer mosses, grasses, lichens, and flowers grow in the tundra.

Lichens have no roots, stems, or leaves. They get their nutrients from the air. This makes lichens very sensitive to pollution in the air. Scientists now study lichens to determine the quality of the air in certain places.

Adaptations make it possible for animals to live in the tundra. Caribou and other mammals develop a thick coat. The hairs of their coats are filled with air. This air insulates the animals from the cold. The caribou's wide hooves help it move easily through the snow in winter or the muddy ground in summer months. Arctic foxes, musk oxen, snowy owls, snowshoe hares, and wolverines also live in the tundra year-round.

Snowy Owl

Wolverine

Caribou

Plants' wide, shallow roots hold them in place so they are not carried away with the icy winds that blow across the arctic tundra.

Many animals live in the tundra for only part of the year. Birds migrate to the tundra to breed. With fewer predators, it is a safer place to raise their young. They find plenty of food in the great number of flies and mosquitoes that breed in the bogs and ponds during the summer months.

4x5 FILM

The ruddy turnstone breeds in the arctic tundra, then migrates south as winter approaches.

In summer, plants grow on the arctic tundra. The permafrost only melts a few inches or centimeters below the surface, though, so no trees or large plants can take root.

Alpine Tundra

High in the mountains lies another type of tundra—the alpine tundra. It is defined more by its elevation than by temperature or rainfall. The alpine tundra begins at the treeline and extends to the mountain peak. The treeline, or timberline, is the altitude at which trees can no longer grow. Animals adapt to these harsh conditions in different ways. Some, like the alpine marmot, hibernate in groups in underground chambers.

Pikas, small mammals related to hares and rabbits, do not hibernate during the winter. They prepare for it throughout the summer, collecting stems and twigs and carrying them back to their territories where they build haystacks in crevices or in the shelter of overhanging rocks.

Alpine tundra

Treeline

CHAPTER FOUR

Grasslands and Chaparral

Grasslands receive about 30 inches (76 centimeters) of rain a year. We find them on every continent except Antarctica. Close to the equator are tropical grasslands. They stay hot year-round. Farther from the equator, temperate grasslands have hot summers and cold winters.

Grasslands go by many names; they are called prairies in North America, pampas in South America, steppes in Europe, and in Africa, they are called savannahs.

In Kenya, the grasslands and mountains of the Great Rift Valley are home to a great variety of animals, including gazelles, hyenas, and lions.

NORTH AMERICA

EUROPE

SOUTH AMERICA

AFRICA

o Kenya

Plants and animals in the grasslands have developed adaptations to help them survive. The stinging nettle plant causes a painful sting when touched. More importantly, its sting protects it from animals that might be tempted to eat it.

The leaves and stems of stinging nettle plants can be used to make medicines and healing teas.

Monarch butterflies have an interesting way of protecting themselves. As larvae, they feed on the milkweed plant. Toxins from the plant remain in the insect's body through its butterfly stage, making it poisonous to predators.

Chaparral

The chaparral is the smallest biome. Like deserts, the chaparral biomes experience summers that are very hot and dry. In the winter, though, they receive more rainfall than deserts, anywhere from 10 to 25 inches (25 to 60 centimeters) a year.

There are different names for the biome, depending on where it is located. In the American West, the name *chaparral* comes from the

Mexican word, *chaparro*, which means *scrub oak*. South Africans call this biome the *fynbos*. In Australia, it is the *mallee scrub*, after a small tree that grows there.

Many types of plants grow in the chaparral, but none of them grows very tall. One way they adapt to the dry conditions is in their root system. Chaparral plants spread their roots out so they can capture as much rain as possible during the winter. They also send their roots deep into the ground so they can absorb groundwater during the dry summer season. Waxy, waterproof leaves help the plants retain moisture.

The California scrub oak provides shade for small animals.

Because chaparral biomes are small, many of the animals also inhabit the biomes that border chaparrals. Jackrabbits live in both the chaparral and the desert. Their large ears help them adapt to the extreme temperatures in these biomes. Jackrabbits will increase or decrease the amount of blood flowing through their ears in order to warm up or cool down.

Jackrabbits eat their food twice. The first time they poop, their feces are soft, green, and rich in vitamins. To get the nutrition and moisture from them, they eat these feces. The second time they poop, their feces are dry and dark brown. The nutrition and moisture are gone, and they leave these feces behind.

With keen vision and a strong sense of smell, coyotes make good hunters.

Many animals in the chaparral are nocturnal. They sleep in underground burrows during the heat of the day and come out at night, when it's cooler, to find food.

Chaparral animals conserve water in interesting ways. The urine of some mice and lizards is a white semi-solid paste. Urinating in this way allows them to keep more water in their bodies.

CHAPTER FIVE

Freshwater Biomes

Freshwater biomes occur as lakes, ponds, rivers, streams, and wetlands. Lakes, ponds, and some wetlands are standing-water ecosystems. Water does not flow in and out of them, but flows within them. This flow of water helps move warmth, oxygen, and nutrients throughout the ecosystem.

Many lakes and ponds have several levels of habitat. Near shore is the littoral zone where cattails and reeds grow in shallow water. Snails, clams, fishes, and amphibians live here.

The upper levels of lakes and ponds receive more sunlight than lower levels. Tiny microorganisms, called plankton, float on the water's surface. There are two types of plankton, phytoplankton and zooplankton.

Cattails benefit ponds and other wetlands by preventing erosion and providing food and shelter for wildlife.

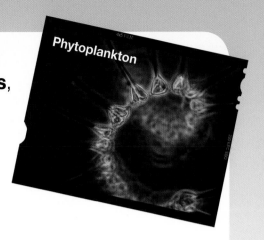

Phytoplankton

In a process called **photosynthesis**, phytoplankton use the Sun's energy to turn water and carbon dioxide into food and oxygen. They are the main **producers** in most water biomes. Zooplankton do not carry out photosynthesis. They are **consumers** in the aquatic ecosystem. Zooplankton feed on phytoplankton, small fish feed on zooplankton, and larger fish feed on smaller fish.

In very deep lakes, sunlight does not reach the deep benthic zone. Many of the organisms living here are scavengers. They feed on the remains of other organisms. Mussels, worms, and barnacles also live in the deep benthic zone.

Water Beetles

Aquatic animals have adaptations that help them survive their environment. Water beetles have to dive for their food. They use hairs under their bodies to trap air so they can breathe under water.

Wetlands

Wetlands are areas of land covered with water for at least part of the year. They are important to the environment. Wetlands remove pollutants from the water that flows through them. They control flooding by absorbing extra water when rivers overflow. They provide spawning grounds for many freshwater fish and habitats for plants and animals.

We did not always understand the importance of wetlands. For years, people drained them so they could build or farm on them. In recent years, as we have begun to understand the role they play in a healthy environment, we have passed laws to protect wetlands.

Common Snipe

American Alligator

Mosquito

The common snipe breeds in Alaska, Canada, and parts of the northern United States, then migrates south for the winter. American alligators do not migrate, but spend their entire lives along the southeast and gulf coasts of the United States.

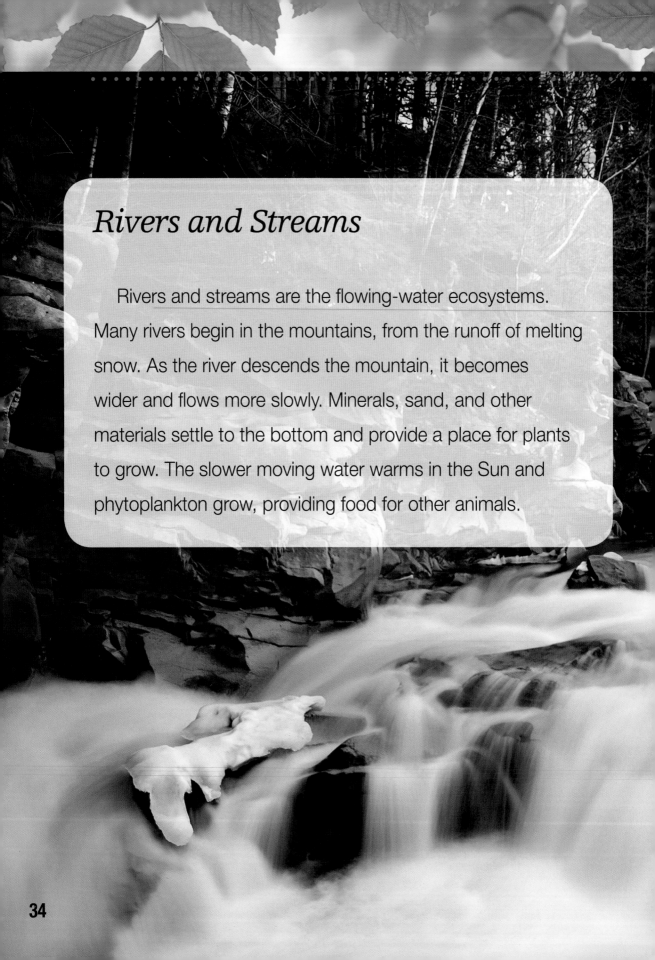

Rivers and Streams

Rivers and streams are the flowing-water ecosystems. Many rivers begin in the mountains, from the runoff of melting snow. As the river descends the mountain, it becomes wider and flows more slowly. Minerals, sand, and other materials settle to the bottom and provide a place for plants to grow. The slower moving water warms in the Sun and phytoplankton grow, providing food for other animals.

Nymph

Dragonfly

There are three stages in the life cycle of a dragonfly; egg, nymph, and adult. Nymphs have a bump on their back, but no wings.

Pollution threatens freshwater biomes. It can come from industry, neighborhoods, or from farms when fertilizers run off from the farmland into rivers and streams. Homeowners are often unaware of the damage they are doing when they dump motor oil or other chemicals into a storm drain.

CHAPTER SIX

Marine Biomes

Marine biomes include all the world's saltwater ecosystems. These are the coastal wetlands, coral reefs, and oceans.

Coastal wetlands are covered by salt water all or part of the time. Many species of fish and wildlife nest and live here. Like freshwater wetlands, they protect areas from flooding, filter pollutants from the water, and provide areas for boating and fishing.

Estuaries are where the freshwater from rivers and streams flows into the saltwater of a marine biome. Estuaries are partially protected from winds and ocean waves by barrier islands or peninsulas.

estuary

220 EPC SSO

Coral Reefs

Coral reefs grow in warm seas. The coral polyp is an animal. As it grows and reproduces, new coral polyps add to the coral reef. Algae settle on the coral and carry out photosynthesis. Small animals eat the algae and in turn are eaten by larger animals. Sea anemones and sponges live on the coral. Many brightly colored fish make their homes here, too. Some have hard mouths and strong teeth, an adaptation that enables them to eat the hard coral.

Bright colors indicate a healthy coral reef.

Clownfish find protection from predators in the tentacles of the sea anemone.

Pollution is a threat to coral reefs. Recreational activity is also a problem. When we drive boats onto reefs or hit them with anchors, we cause severe damage to the ecosystem. Additionally, rising water temperatures are putting stress on the ecosystem, causing the release of the colorful algae that live on coral. Once this happens, the coral loses its color, becoming white. This coral bleaching is a sign that the reef is in trouble. If it continues, the colony can die, but if the stressful conditions reverse it is possible for the reef to recover.

Oceans

Earth's oceans cover about 70 percent of its surface. The Pacific Ocean alone covers almost half of Earth's surface. Oceans are deep. Their average depth is more than 2 miles (3.5 kilometers). Powerful currents keep the water in the oceans moving. Waves crash at the shorelines. The pull of the Moon causes daily high and low tides. The ocean itself is home to over 1 million species of plants and animals, and there are many more yet to be discovered.

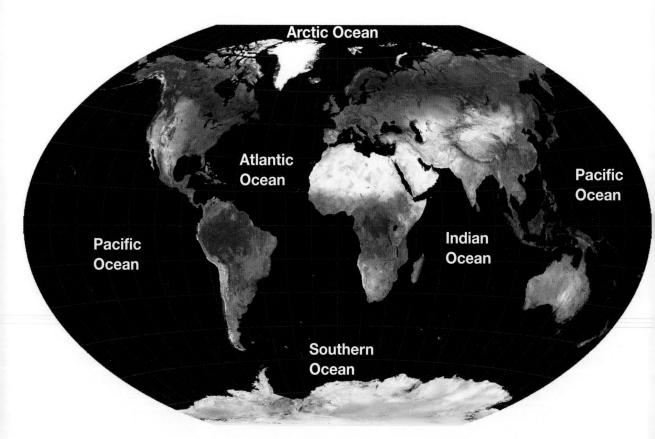

Marine plants and algae are important to life in water and on land. Through photosynthesis, they take in huge amounts of carbon dioxide and produce much of the world's oxygen supply. Seaweeds are the largest algae. They absorb their food from the water. They do not have roots. Instead, they live attached to rocks and other objects.

Kelp are a type of seaweed that grow in cold, nutrient-rich water. They depend on sunlight for photosynthesis. Kelp grows in large groups called kelp forests, where they provide food and shelter for a wide variety of animals.

Overfishing and Pollution Threaten Oceans

For thousands of years, man has gathered food from the oceans. In the past hundred years, fishing has become more efficient. Commercial fishing boats use electronic equipment to locate and scoop up whole schools of fish. This practice has nearly wiped out some species of fish in the northeast Atlantic. There are quotas to prevent commercial fishermen from taking too many fish at one time, but the quotas are too high. More needs to be done before some species are destroyed altogether.

There is great biodiversity in the Earth's oceans. The largest mammal on Earth, the blue whale, feeds on tiny shrimplike animals called krill. The largest fish, the whale shark, can grow to 46 feet (14 meters) long.

Whale Shark

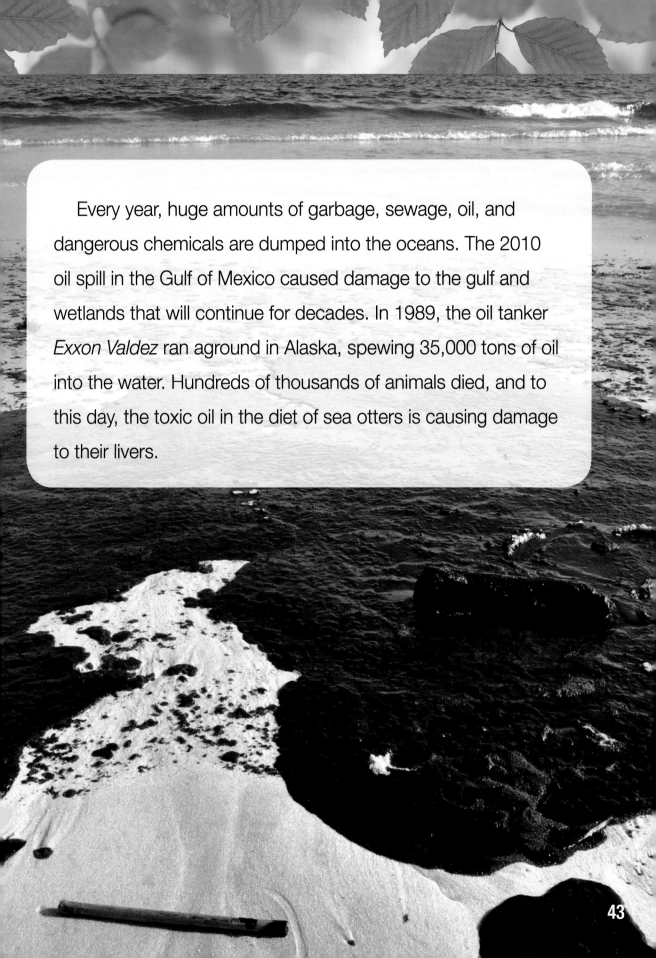

Every year, huge amounts of garbage, sewage, oil, and dangerous chemicals are dumped into the oceans. The 2010 oil spill in the Gulf of Mexico caused damage to the gulf and wetlands that will continue for decades. In 1989, the oil tanker *Exxon Valdez* ran aground in Alaska, spewing 35,000 tons of oil into the water. Hundreds of thousands of animals died, and to this day, the toxic oil in the diet of sea otters is causing damage to their livers.

CHAPTER SEVEN

Caring for the Earth

All plants and animals depend on healthy biomes. With a little effort, we can help.

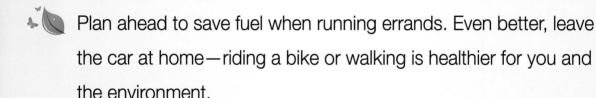 Plan ahead to save fuel when running errands. Even better, leave the car at home—riding a bike or walking is healthier for you and the environment.

Recycle to save resources and fuel.

Keep hazardous chemicals out of the water supply by taking them to the proper place to recycle them.

Get to know your biome. Do you know the plants and animals that live there? The more you know, the better you can appreciate your place in the natural world.

Try This!

BUILD A BACKYARD ECOSYSTEM

You can create a backyard habitat for the animals that live in your community. Choose a good spot to plant some native plants and shrubs to provide protection and food for wildlife. Be careful to find out if the plants you choose require full sunlight or shade during the day.

Next, add a water source for insects, birds, or other wildlife that might visit. Add seed for birds, and nuts for squirrels and other small animals. If you hope to attract butterflies, add a flat area where water can pool. You can also find out which plants are most attractive to the butterflies in your area.

Stay away from toxic pesticides and weed killers which will cause harm to the animal life in your habitat.

Keep a log of the various birds, insects, and small animals that visit your backyard ecosystem. Do you see some unfamiliar faces? You might want to check out a field guide to learn more about them.

Glossary

adaptations (ad-ap-TAY-shuhnz): changes in plants and animals that help them live better in their environment

altitude (AL-ti-tood): the height of something above sea level

aquatic (uh-KWAT-ik): having to do with water

biodiversity (bye-oh-duh-VURS-it-ee): a wide variety of species in a region

consumers (kuhn-SOO-murz): animals that eat other animals or plants

deforestation (dee-for-ist-AY-shuhn): permanent removal of the trees in a forest

equator (i-KWAY-tur): the imaginary line around the middle of the Earth that is halfway between the north and south poles

latitude (LAT-uh-tood): the location of a place, measured in degrees north or south of the equator

microorganisms (mye-kroh-OR-guh-niz-uhmz): living things so small they can only be seen with a microscope

photosynthesis (foh-toh-SIN-thuh-siss): the process where plants use energy from the Sun to turn water and carbon dioxide into food and oxygen

precipitation (pri-sip-i-TAY-shuhn): water that falls from the sky as rain, sleet, hail, or snow

producers (pruh-DOOSS-urz): organisms that take the Sun's energy and turn it into energy for themselves and for consumers

taproot (TAP-root): a large central root from which smaller roots grow

temperate (TEM-pur-it): a region with temperatures that are not extremely high or low

terrestrial (tuh-RESS-tree-uhl): having to do with the Earth

Index

Websites to Visit

www.kids.nceas.ucsb.edu/biomes/index.html

www.kidskonnect.com/subject-index/15-science/62-biomes.html

www.worldbiomes.com/

www.cybersleuth-kids.com/sleuth/Science/Earth_Science/Biomes/

www.mbgnet.net/

About the Author

Jeanne Sturm grew up exploring the woods, waterfalls, and riverbanks around her home in Chagrin Falls, Ohio. She earned her Education degree at Bowling Green State University and moved to Tampa, Florida, to teach. She began windsurfing, where she met her future husband. Now married, Jeanne, her husband, and their three children live in Land O' Lakes, Florida, with their dog, Astro.